HEROES AND ANTI HEROES

HEROES
AND
ANTI
HEROES

INTRODUCTION BY JOHN UPDIKE

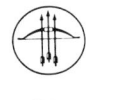

André Deutsch

First published in Great Britain in 1991
by André Deutsch Limited
105-106 Great Russell Street, London WC1B 3LJ

Photographs © Magnum Photos 1991
Introduction © John Updike 1991
All rights reserved.
Design by Barney Wan

British Library Cataloguing in Publication Data
A catalogue record for this book is available
from the British Library.

ISBN 0 233 98628 6

Printed in Singapore by
Kim Hup Lee Printing Co Pte Ltd.

MAGNUM *Images*

INTRODUCTION BY JOHN UPDIKE

CHE GUEVARA *Elliott Erwitt 1964*

MAO on Long March *Anon. 1935*

MAO & DENG *New China Pictures 1975*

The post-war era, with its intricate avoidance of global holocaust and its many shades of political grey, has not conduced to the creation of heroes and anti-heroes. Che Guevara, for instance, would seem to have been a hero to the photographer Elliott Erwitt, who caught his youthful and lightly bearded face bathed in the unabashed radiance of Hollywood publicity stills, but to others he was, as he seems in the image by René Burri, a tousled-haired kid mischievously playing at soldier while brandishing a cigar in imitation of his big brother. Mao Tse-tung projected a heroic image, all right, which we can see in its Long March guise and in its head-of-state maturity. But, since the great Chairman's demise, revulsion has been expressed within China as well as without at some of his revolutionary measures, and the moment when Mao was an idol to university students from Berkeley to Burma seems forever by. We are attracted, rather, as 'truer to life', to the unposed profile captured with Deng Xiaoping, in which the Chairman seems curiously soft and semi-formed, chinless and doll-like. A still-living political figure frequently caught in Magnum's focus is the irrepressibly pop-eyed and chronically unshaven Yasser Arafat, with a heap of striped cloth spilling from his head; it is hard to picture any turn in world events which will make him appear, visually, heroic.

Faces tell us less about good and evil than we imagine. Much of our response to an image of a personality is pre-conditioned. Without knowing anything of these men's history, we might pick Klaus Barbie as the most distinguished and benign physiognomy the book holds, and we would certainly be touched by the tender images of Stalin carrying his young daughter Svetlana and Hitler reaching out to the little girl who has apparently just given him a bouquet. There are not many evil-looking men in this volume, and most of them are American Presidents – Nixon as a black-hatted gangster, Johnson and Humphrey posed behind the podium in a sly clench of dissimulation, Herbert Hoover

GODFREY MOLOI, Soweto gangster *Gideon Mendel 1988*

exuding white-tie arrogance as millions stand in breadlines. The handsomest men, to my eye, are not the movie stars but the industrialist Giovanni Agnelli, South Africa's Minister of Foreign Affairs Pik Botha and the pro-Nazi magnate Alfred Krupp, with his industrious minions and Mephisthophelean glower. The ugliest, most grotesquely creased and reptilian visage herein belongs to the book's one saint, Mother Theresa, and the sunniest-looking man is Godfrey Moloi of Soweto, a convicted murderer and successful black racketeer.

If our era has trouble generating heroes and anti-heroes, the

SADAT & ARAFAT *Rene Burri 1974*

11

HERBERT HOOVER *Erich Salomon 1932*

STALIN *Collection Astier 1933*

JOMO KENYATTA *Ian Berry 1961*

camera is one of the reasons – along with television and the endlessly prying free press, it brings us too close to our living leaders and artistic stars, shows us their moles, their dewlaps, their foolish flashbulbed on-camera grins and their shifty eyes and full mouths in moments of violated privacy. We see they are not icons. In the olden days of monarchies, royal images circulated only as profiles on coins, and nothing was minted that would interfere with the smoothness of the regal transmission of messages and good fortune from Divinity Itself. When I was in college, T. S. Eliot was represented in anthologies almost invariably by the same expressionless profile; my friend and colleague Philip Roth repeats the same stern photograph on jacket after jacket with a kindred sacralising effect. Throughout the Soviet empire, in its pre-Gorbachev tranquillity, the image of Lenin was distributed very widely but with a distinct narrowness of expression and pointed sameness of salient attributes – the jaunty goatee, the bald dome, the steely gaze with its bead on the coming workers' paradise. It is an image all edges, with which to slice up the future.

PIK BOTHA *Gideon Mendel 1986*

Some of these Magnum images, often those we have seen reproduced before, do present an iconic force, a realer-than-real crystallisation that stamps itself on our memory. Camus, Matisse and Faulkner by Cartier-Bresson, Mishima by Elliott Erwitt, Jomo Kenyatta by Ian Berry, Billy Graham by Arnold, Cocteau by Halsmann, Sartre and Simone de Beauvoir by Barbey and a wailing Joplin by Elliot Landy, a wonderfully puzzled-looking Einstein by Ernst Haas. Cornell Capa caught a doubly iconic image of President John Kennedy and, in foreboding foreground profile, his successor Lyndon Johnson, with the Presidential seal in central focus. Our knowledge of the abrupt assassination that will in an instant transfer the power of the seal from one man to the other enters into the photograph, and becomes part of its aesthetic force. Would Gilles Peress's dramatically shadowed portrait

CHARLES DE GAULLE *Erich Lessing 1958*

of Salman Rushdie strike us quite so strongly without our knowledge of the engulfing shadows that have subsequently hidden this author from sight? A few very photogenic men, like Rushdie, Churchill, and the Ayatollah Khomeini, are consistently iconic in the image they project. In the photograph by Abbas, the Ayatollah looms above the dowdy other Iranians in the photo with a higher order of vividness – so much so that we check his edges to make sure he is not a cardboard cut-out, a mounted poster.

We live in an age of images, of signs. Castro's beard and cigar, Khrushchev's bald head seen from behind, De Gaulle's *képi* seen from above are enough to identify them. Charlie Mingus and Pablo Casals are subsumed in the stringed instruments they mastered. The reality and the image become interchangeable: Anwar Sadat is hidden by microphones but his iconic self stands forth above his head; Jesse Jackson's exuberant arms-up gesture occurs simultaneously with its broadcast version on television. Guy Le Querrec very wittily captures the business of image-making in operation, as he shows Mitterrand reading the newspaper while the sculptor extracts his head from the cerebral activity and from the tangled heroics on the tapestry behind him. In a number of portraits a peculiar poignance is generated by the juxtaposition of a living person with a visual artifact – Borges and a blind-looking bust, Picasso looking angry and stunted next to a slave by

NIKITA KRUSCHEV *Burt Glinn 1959*

J L BORGES *Ferdinando Scianna 1984*

CHARLIE MINGUS *Guy Le Querrec 1976*

ADOLF HITLER *W Vandivert 1932*

Michelangelo, Berenson looking beatific over the hip of a reposing Venus. And whose heart would not soften toward Mrs Thatcher, seeing her sitting with such demure reserve, such curious girlish melancholy in juxtaposition with the image of her masculine model in tenacity and Toryism?

Though the camera can catch indelible images, its basic procedures work against heroism. It has a democratic and inclusive eye; it is no respecter of celebrities. Again and again, studying these pictures of the famous, our eyes go to the side, to the faces caught by accident in the frame. Nasser and Castro, at the height of their pride as Third-World gadflies and glamour-boys, walk down a street in New York, and it is the deadpan policemen guarding them, and the sullen anonymous faces pressed into the telephoto shot with them, that pique our curiosity. Elsewhere, Sadat and Arafat sit upon a stage; are those watchful men behind them the bodyguards who will so dismally fail to

MARGARET THATCHER *Eve Arnold 1987*

NASSER & CASTRO at the United Nations *Bob Henriques 1960*

NIKITA KRUSCHEV & SHIRLEY MACLAINE
in Hollywood *Bob Henriques 1959*

protect Sadat not long hereafter? President Nkrumah of Ghana shakes hands with an African chief, but our eye goes to the wary young face between them, with his tilted pillbox hat and embroidered kaftan and elegant eye-whites. Khrushchev, ruler of world Communism, comes to Hollywood, and it is the perky actress, a girlish Shirley MacLaine, daring to pat his bald forehead whom the camera 'loves', as they say – her, and the amiably bored Louis Jourdan gazing off the photograph's edge. Who is that man stepping out so smartly behind Adolf Hitler? Who are those chunky giggling women flanking Yuri Gagarin? Who, for

ALBERT SCHWEITZER *George Rodger 1951*

YURI GAGARIN *Seymour Raskin 1963*

JAMES DEAN *Dennis Stock 1955*

that matter, is the young dog stretching itself behind William Faulkner's back, and that kitten on Albert Schweitzer's wrist? Our eye, like a kitten, is drawn toward the liveliest spot on a photograph, the spot in motion, and that is often not the subject's face. The portrait painter of old directed our attention along the proper flow-lines, and combed superfluous energy out of the canvas. As on a theatrical stage, everything in the painting was a prop, with its assured use.

But a photograph can't help taking in the surroundings, the setting, and these trappings can frame the hero in absurdity. The pope dwarfed by his limousine, the Shah by his throne and robes, Hirohito by the stadium into which he is emerging like a mole in a morning coat - the comedy of grand eminence makes us irreverent. Eichmann and his empty chair, surrounded by curtains like a terrible contaminant, arouses another emotion, a Beckettian dread, an inkling of deadly emptiness. James Dean asleep before a floodlit mansion out of cinematic dreamland, Nelson Rockefeller good-naturedly coping with the garbagy indignation of some constituents – these images also have a surreal aptness. Politicians usually work in a crowd, and musicians too; there is a natural pictographic drama that, for Herbert von Karajan and Josephine Baker, comes with the job. And it seems effortlessly fitting, too, to capture Walt Disney in Disneyland, Dr Spock with a child, and Churchill on a landing craft. Landscape, oddly, figures in rather few of these images; the great and famous function mostly in cities. Pasternak sulking at Peredelkino and the Nixons throwing bizarre shadows among the Pyramids do set off Nature to some effect, engendering a visual subtext concerning space and freedom. Nixon, Pasternak, in their different ways, are not free.

The concept of heroism belongs to a world of black and white, a world that ebbed after 1945. Once colour became the rule for Hollywood motion pictures, they ceased to throw off stars with the

NELSON ROCKEFELLER *Charles Gatewood 1970*

WALT DISNEY *Wayne Miller 1955*

EMPEROR HIROHITO *Marc Riboud 1958*

NIXON & SADAT *René Burri 1974*

lambent crispness and marmoreal beauty of Gable, Cooper, Crawford, Garbo, and those dozens of other divinities etched on the skyey screen in platinum and carbon. And once peace, however uneasy, descended upon the globe, heroes and anti-heroes became harder to find. To anyone with a memory of World War Two, heroism and wickedness – good and evil embodied – are live categories. Heroes abounded, from the RAF pilots of the Battle of Britain to the Marines and infantrymen who fell to Axis bullets at Guadalcanal and Stalingrad. The leaders of that epic conflict were heroic – Churchill and Roosevelt both ringingly eloquent, unflinchingly self-confident, lordly in their righteousness as they opposed the diabolical and implacable Hitler, whose black deeds outraced even the calumnies of war propaganda, for the vast thoroughness of his Final Solution, and his final frenzied disregard of the German people he had led into hell, were not fully revealed until the war had ended. Around Hitler a rabble of lesser devils teemed, as colourful as comic-book villains – fat vain Goering, tiny shrill Goebbels, pale wispy Himmler, drooling anti-Semites like Streicher, crazy men like Hess, unbending merciless monocled Prussian generals, not to mention that ridiculous bully Mussolini and the sub-human Japanese automatons under Tojo. Even at the hottest passages of the Cold War – Greece, Korea, the Berlin Blockade, the Cuban Missile Crisis, the various spy trials and exposés, Vietnam, Afghanistan – devil-theories did not dominate diplomatic relations nor, I believe, the popular mentality. Perhaps Americans had too recently, in the war against Hitler, seen the Russians as fellow-heroes to cast them as anti-heroes. And there was something disarming, on both sides, about the geographical amplitude both the superpowers enjoyed, with so much of the world, except at the Bering Strait, between them. And of course the fact of atomic weapons was a great inhibitor. For whatever combination of reasons, real enmity – the sanctioned hatred and black-and-white stylisation that the war spirit needs – never existed between the Russians and Americans. They had seen too many of our movies, perhaps, and we had read too many of their novels. Stalin, for all the rumoured and real atrocities he inflicted upon the Soviet people, was a somewhat ambiguous figure, with a twinkle in his eye and a curve to his moustache. The 1923 photograph of the newly elected Secretary General captures a curious delicacy, an abstracted distance. The odour of idealistic intentions never quite left him. Khrushchev, even while he was banging his shoe and threatening to bury us, was lovable, really, and Brezhnev seemed a good old boy, a

SHAH OF IRAN *Marilyn Silverstone 1962*

JOHN PAUL II *Eugene Richards 1979*

21

GENERAL JARUZELSKI *Bruno Barbey 1981*

crafty power broker with whom Nixon felt more camaraderie than with most Americans. Nixon has recently become the hero of an opera, and his kind of heroism – a knot of inner conflicts, tensions, and contradictions projected onto the worldwide publicity screen – is what the post-war years can offer. Gorbachev could be cast as such a hero, but not Reagan.

As the Cold War melts, consider a personage like General Wojciech Jaruzelski, photographed at stiff attention by Bruno Barbey. Hero? Not to us, or to most Poles. Anti-hero, then? Well, it could be said that he took the steps necessary to save Poland from losing what independence she had at the time, and without which there would be no transition to the better, freer Poland that seems on the way. His face is a prim and rather blank face, a bit like Eichmann's, a bit like Jean Genet's. Its moral shade is as in-between as the tint of his sunglasses. The faces of political leaders almost never look evil, because all leaders think they are doing the right thing. A private individual, raised with the Ten Commandments and a bourgeois superego, may experience guilt over some actions, and the steady self-dislike that warps a visage; an artist might be painfully conscious of plagiarism and selling out, and grow a visible cloud on his expression. But national leaders, immersed in contending pressures, faced daily with choices all of which have a 'down side' adversely affecting thousands if not millions, can commit mistakes but not, in the realm of their decision-making, sins. Even Hitler's plunges into genocide figured in his mind as measures beneficial to his chosen constituency, the German 'Aryan' people. We have no photograph here of Pol Pot, but if there were one, his face would no doubt be serene, numbed by the chloroform of sincere doctrine and settled policy. The most murderous leader in this volume, Hitler and Stalin and Mao excepted, must be Idi Amin, and it is true that, as photographed by Abbas, he does look menacing, and his uniform megalomaniacal. Yet his predecessor and successor, Dr Milton Obote, wears a menace of his own, and in fact both men permitted and urged horrors in the miserable history of cruel warfare among the tribes of Uganda.

History, as we now conceive it, is anti-heroic – a matter, for historians of the annalist school, of the little anonymous lives, of market records and statistics, of life-styles and technology. The study of 'great men' savours now of the barbaric, the credulous, the regressive. No more Napoleons, no more Davids to paint them on horseback. Instead, grindingly dull memoirs as an eventual fruit of office, and in the meantime a mob of paparazzi popping away during photo opportunities.

It may be better so. Heroes and anti-heroes are created by our need for them; this need arises in times of emergency, despair, and martial rallying. If we, and the cameras in the skilful hands of Magnum's world-roving photographers, see relatively few of them around, the paucity should not be too loudly mourned. The times that breed heroes are generally grim times for the unheroic multitudes. A reluctance to confer the adoration that makes heroes, and to feel a blind hatred for opponents and rivals, augurs a growth of judiciousness and empathy within the run of mankind, and an advance for the civic co-existence that we all, on this shrinking planet, must try to shape.

SAUL STEINBERG & FRIENDS *Inge Morath 1962*

Overleaf: MIKHAIL GORBACHEV & RONALD REAGAN *Peter Marlow 1985*

RICHARD NIXON *Elliott Erwitt 1955*

LEONID BREZHNEV *Raghu Rai 1980*

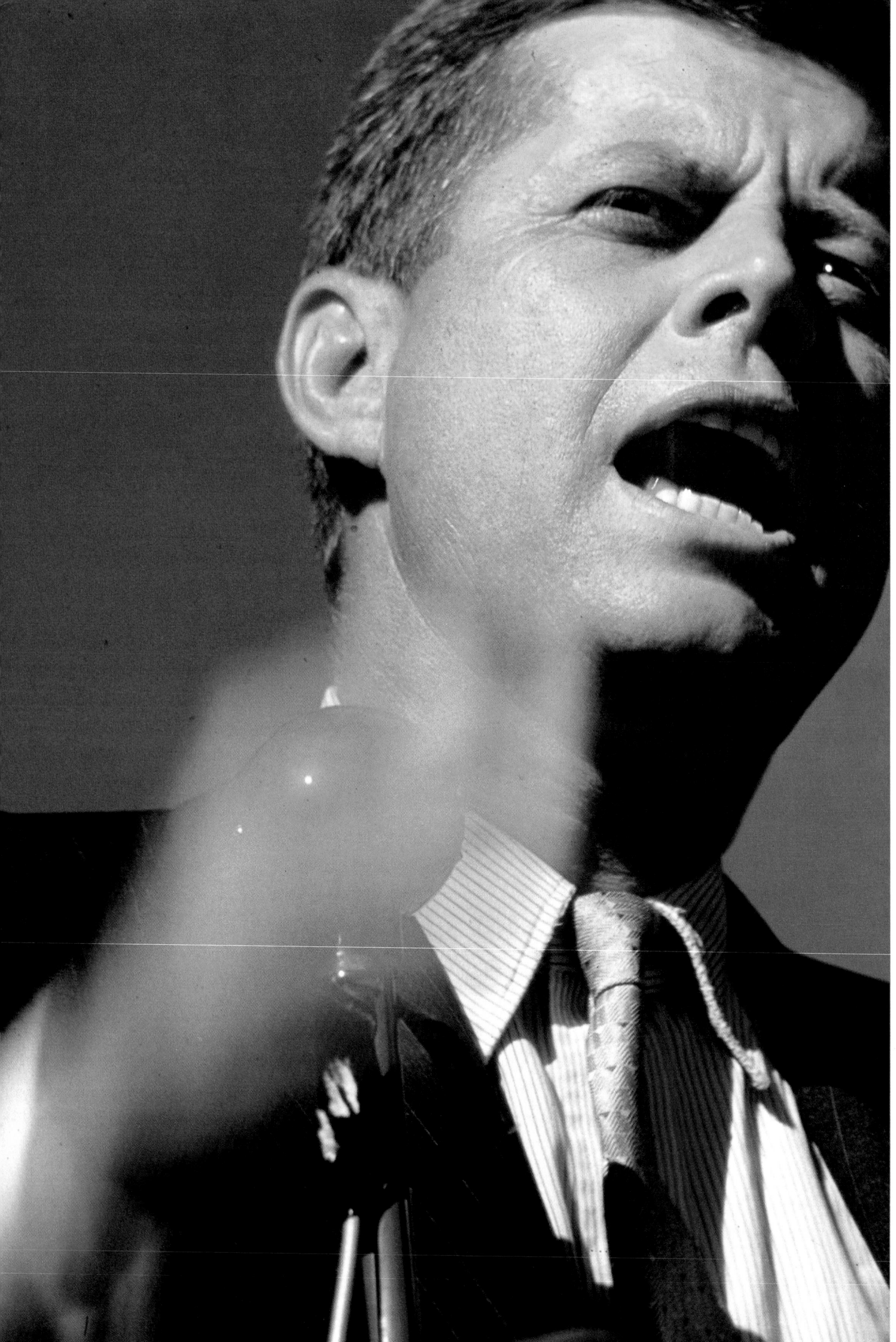

FIDEL CASTRO *Burt Glinn 1959*

JOHN F KENNEDY *Cornell Capa 1960*

31

JOSEF STALIN AT POTSDAM CONFERENCE *Ye Haldei 1945*

IKE & MAMIE EISENHOWER *Burt Glinn 1961*

LECH WALESA *Jean Gaumy 1980*

NICOLAE CEAUSESCU *Abbas 1982*

35

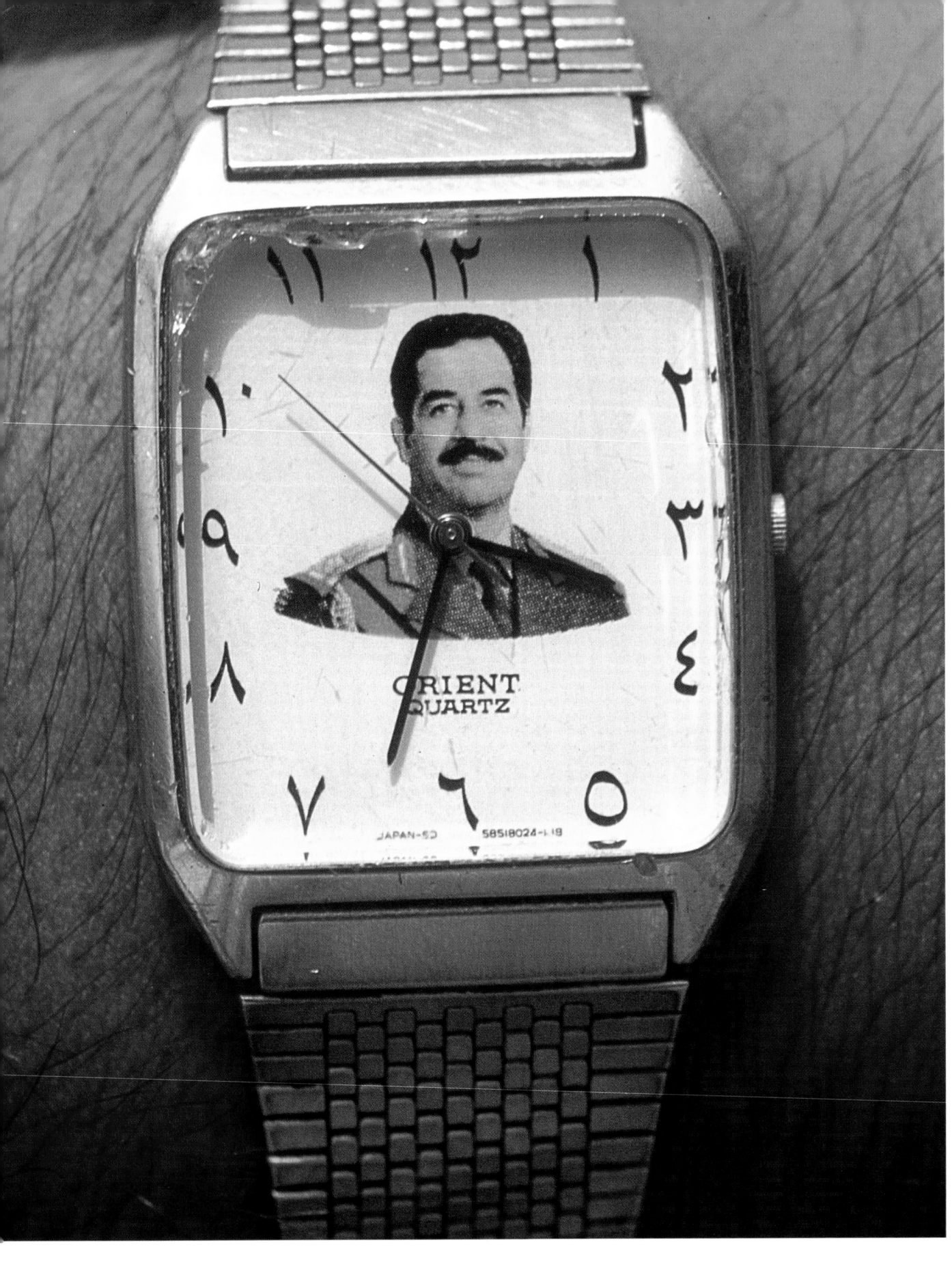

SADDAM HUSSEIN *Steve McCurry 1983*

GEORGE BUSH *Alex Webb 1988*

DANIEL ORTEGA WITH SANDINO MURAL *Susan Meiselas 1984*

FERDINAND MARCOS *Steve McCurry 1985*

38

GORBACHEV & LENIN *Abbas 1988*

MOHAMMAD ZIA UL HAQ *Abbas 1988*

39

SALVADOR ALLENDE *Bruno Barbey 1973*

GENERAL PINOCHET *Susan Meiselas 1988*

Previous page: ANASTASIO SOMOZA *Susan Meiselas 1979*

43

YOUTHS PRACTISE THROWING CONTACT BOMBS, NICARAGUA *Susan Meiselas 1978*

CHE GUEVARA *René Burri 1963*

Opposite: CHRISTOPHER REEVE AS SUPERMAN *Burt Glinn 1979*

Overleaf: RICHARD NIXON *Raymond Depardon 1968*

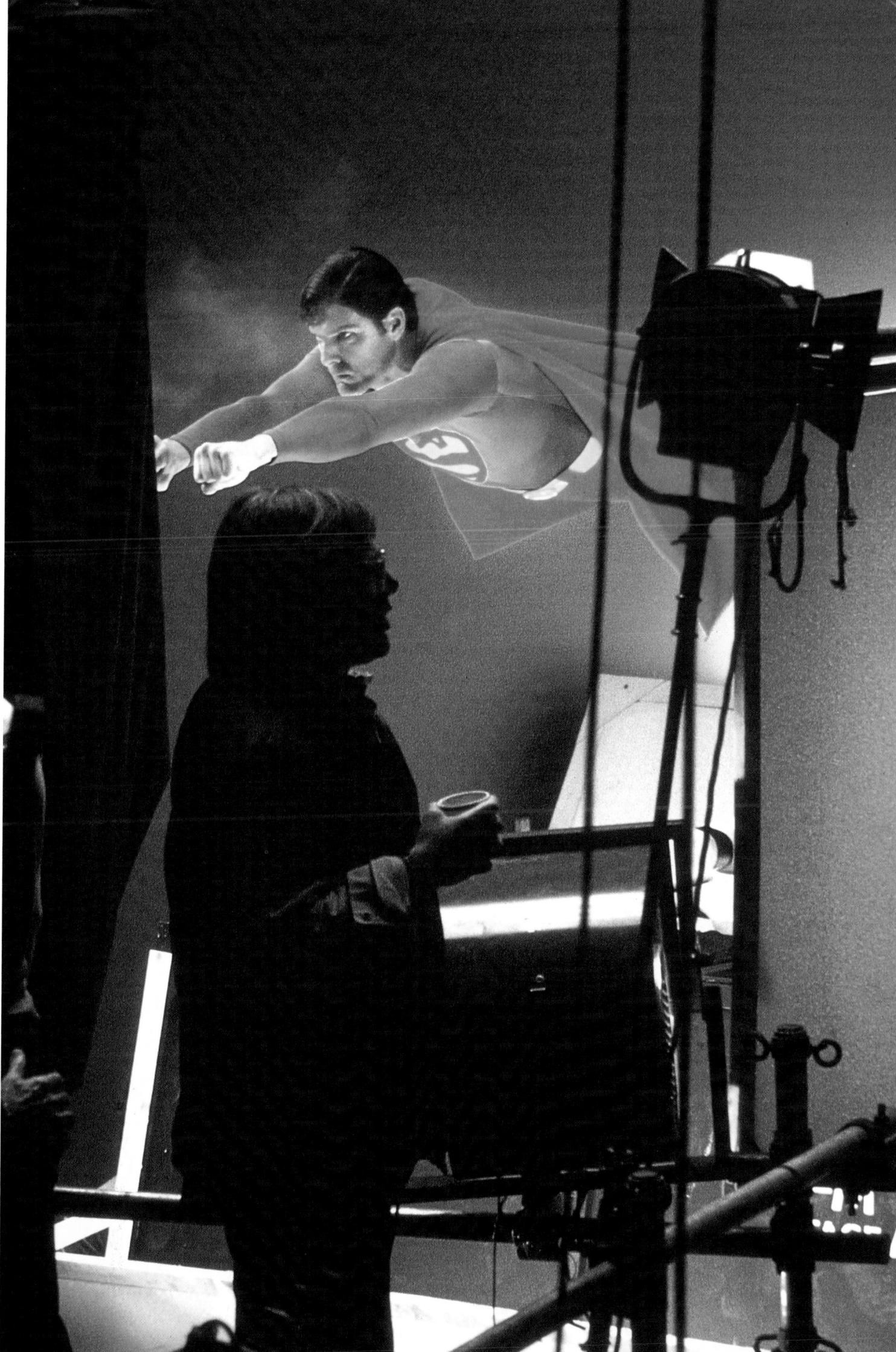

MARTIN LUTHER KING *Leonard Freed 1963*

JOHN F KENNEDY *Cornell Capa 1961*

53

JACKIE KENNEDY *Eve Arnold 1960*

CORETTA KING AT MARTIN LUTHER KING'S FUNERAL *Costa Manos 1968*

GERALD FORD *Gilles Peress 1976*

LYNDON B JOHNSON & HUBERT HUMPHREY *Bob Adelman 1968*

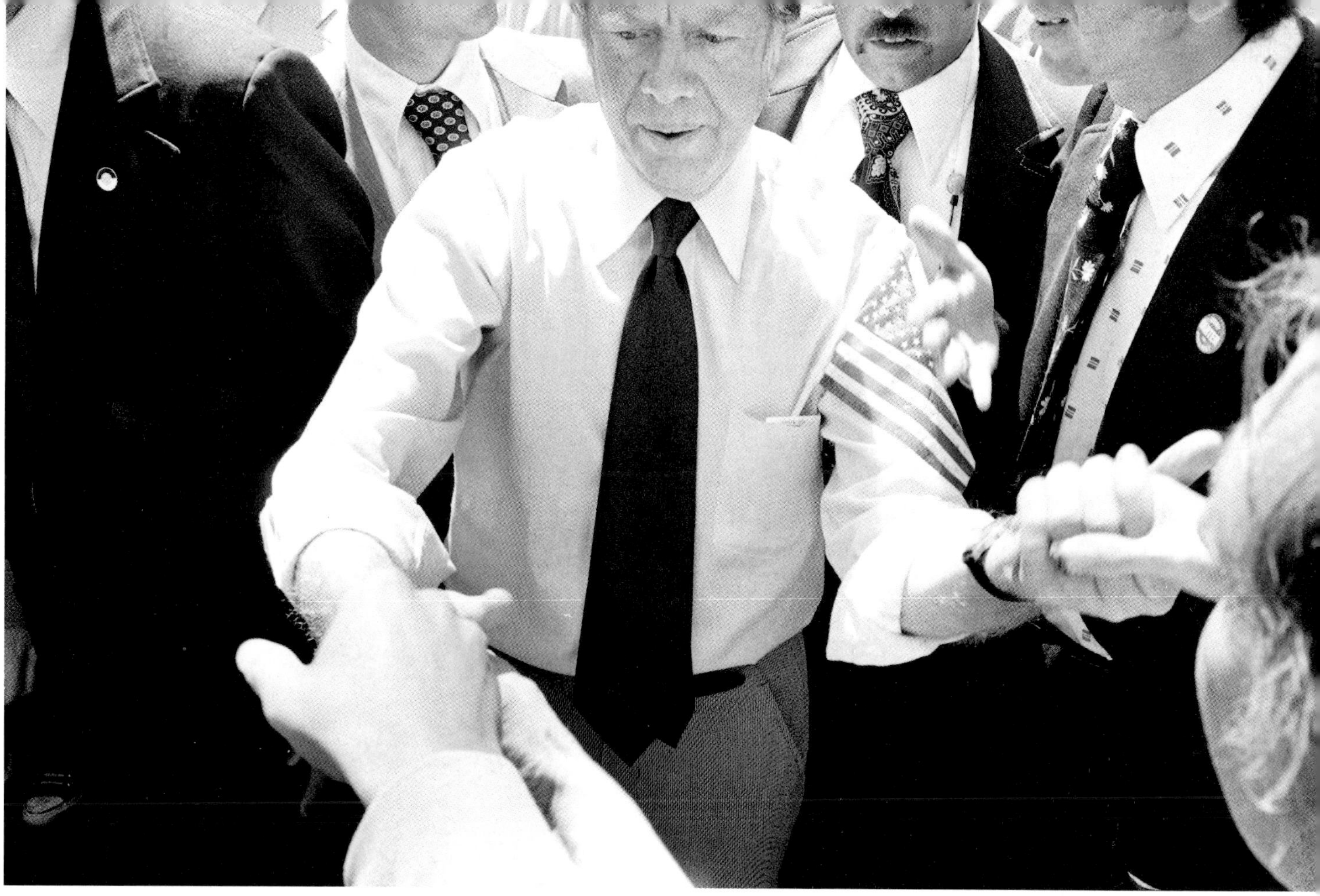

JIMMY CARTER *Gilles Peress 1976*

TOGETHER... A NEW BEGINNING

BARBARA & GEORGE BUSH, RONALD & NANCY REAGAN *Alex Webb 1980*

ANWAR SADAT *Micha Bar'am 1977*

MENACHEM BEGIN *Robert Capa 1950*

GOLDA MEIR *Micha Bar'am 1970*

DAVID BEN GURION *Marilyn Silverstone 1964*

FUNERAL OF NASSER *Bruno Barbey 1970*

ARIEL SHARON & MOSHE DAYAN *Micha Bar'am 1973*

KWAME NKRUMAH *Marc Riboud 1960*

WILLY BRANDT *Thomas Hoepker 1967*

JEAN BEDEL BOKASSA *Abbas 1977*

IDI AMIN *Abbas 1973*

HENDRIK VERWOERD *Ian Berry 1961*

NELSON MANDELA *Ian Berry 1961*

P W BOTHA *Gideon Mendel 1987*

BENAZIR BHUTTO *Abbas 1988*

MRS BANDARANAIKE *Bruno Barbey 1977*

JAWAHARLAL NEHRU *Ernst Haas 1955*

INDIRA GANDHI *Marilyn Silverstone 1971*

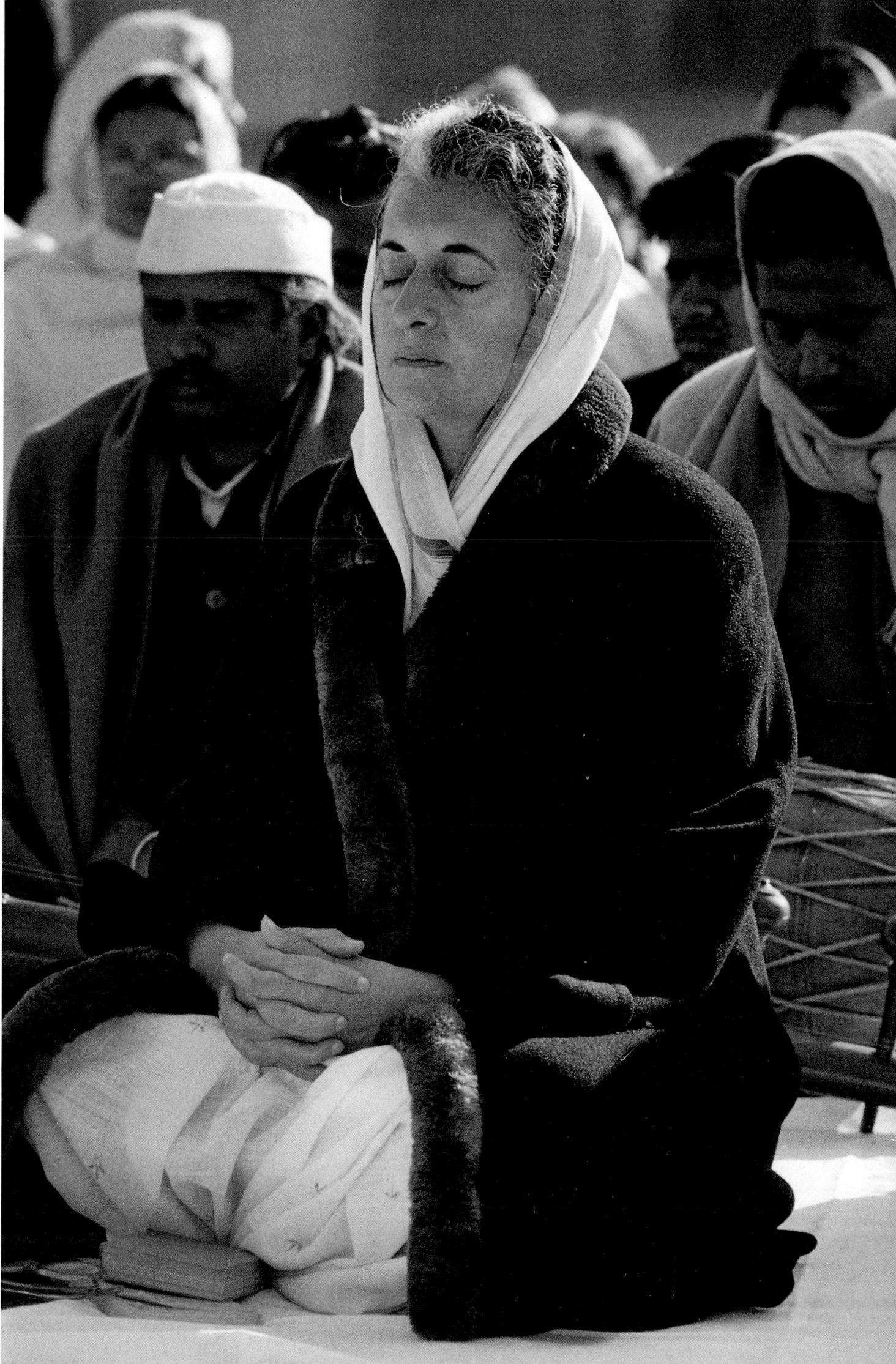

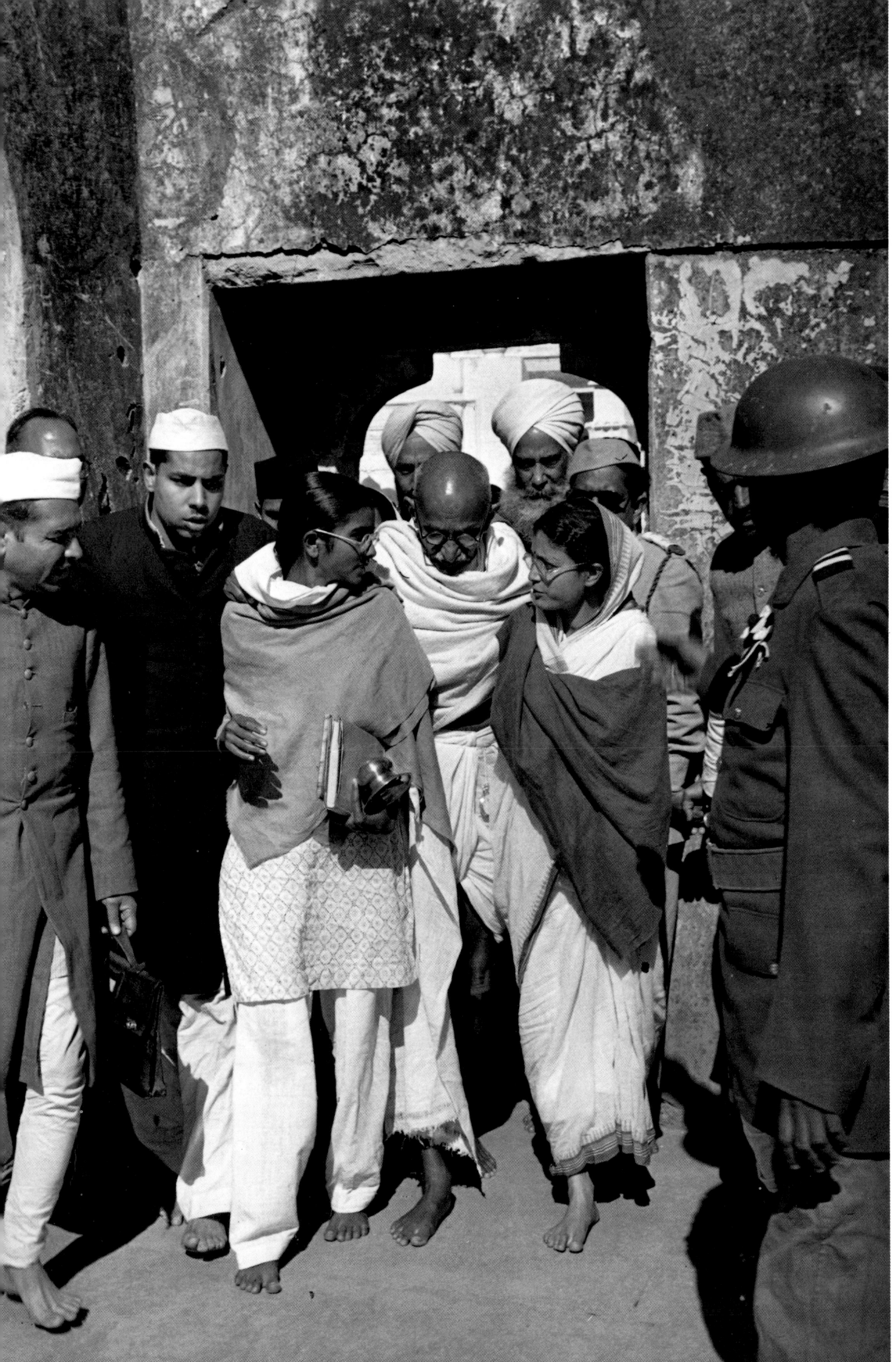

FUNERAL OF MAHATMA GANDHI *Henri Cartier-Bresson 1948*

MAHATMA GANDHI *Henri Cartier-Bresson 1948*

79

ALBERT SCHWEITZER *Eugene Smith 1949*

MOTHER THERESA *Raghu Rai 1987*

CARL JUNG *Henri Cartier-Bresson*

BERTRAND RUSSELL *Marc Riboud*

JESSE JACKSON *Eli Reed 1984*

Previous page: POPE PAUL VI *Marc Riboud 1972*

BILLY GRAHAM *Cornell Capa 1947*

DALAI LAMA *Raghu Rai 1987*

MAHARASHI YOGI *Philippe Halsman*

JOHN PAUL II *Gilles Peress 1979*

KU KLUX KLAN RALLY *Alex Webb 1979*

JEAN-MARIE LE PEN *Abbas 1986*

JOHN TYNDALL *Peter Marlow 1977*

E is NO GOD BUT ALLA

MALCOLM X *Eve Arnold 1961*

LINCOLN ROCKWELL *Eve Arnold 1961*

Overleaf: JAMES BALDWIN *Marc Riboud 1962*

JANE FONDA *Marc Riboud 1972*

VANESSA REDGRAVE *David Hurn 1968*

JAMES DEAN *Dennis Stock 1955*

JAMES DEAN *Dennis Stock 1955*

103

MARILYN MONROE *Eve Arnold 1960*

SOPHIA LOREN *David Seymour 1955*

BRIGITTE BARDOT *Philippe Halsman 1950*

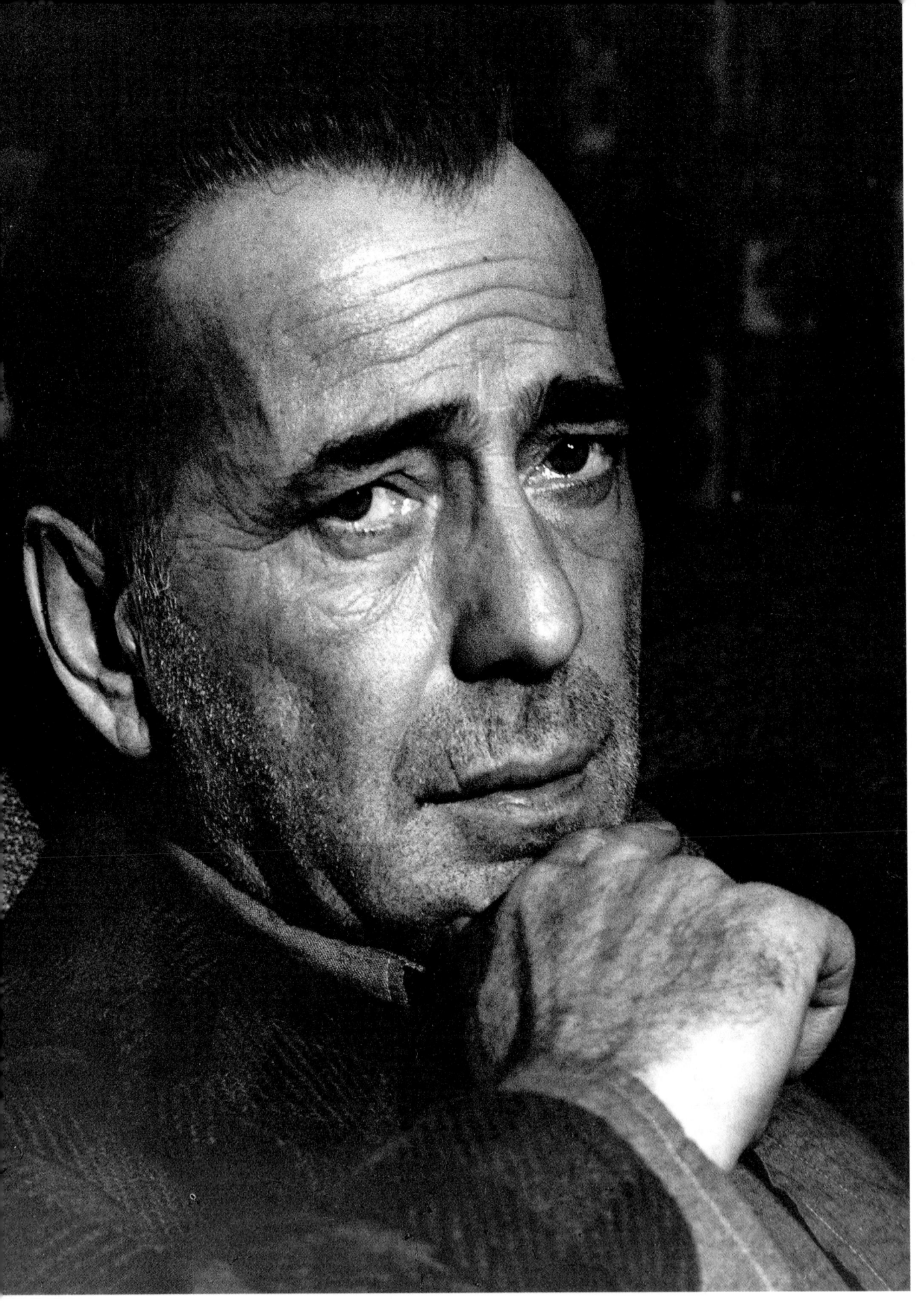

HUMPHREY BOGART *Elliott Erwitt*

MARLON BRANDO *Philippe Halsman*

PRINCESS GRACE OF MONACO *Elliott Erwitt 1956*

INGRID BERGMAN AND HER TWIN DAUGHTERS ISABELLA & INGRID ROSSELLINI *David Seymour 1952*

RICHARD BURTON & ELIZABETH TAYLOR *Eve Arnold 1963*

Previous page: ALFRED HITCHCOCK *Philippe Halsman 1962*

JEAN-LOUIS BARRAULT *René Burri 1956*

SIMONE SIGNORET & YVES MONTAND *Dennis Stock 1960*

CLARK GABLE *Eve Arnold 1960*

WOODY ALLEN *Gilles Peress 1980*

AKIRA KUROSAWA *René Burri 1961*

JEAN GENET *Henri Cartier-Bresson 1963*

YUKIO MISHIMA *Elliott Erwitt 1970*

ALBERT CAMUS *Henri Cartier-Bresson 1944*

SIMONE DE BEAUVOIR & JEAN-PAUL SARTRE *Bruno Barbey 1969*

EZRA POUND *Henri Cartier-Bresson 1970*

JOHN STEINBECK *Robert Capa 1947*

131

ERNEST HEMINGWAY *Robert Capa 1941*

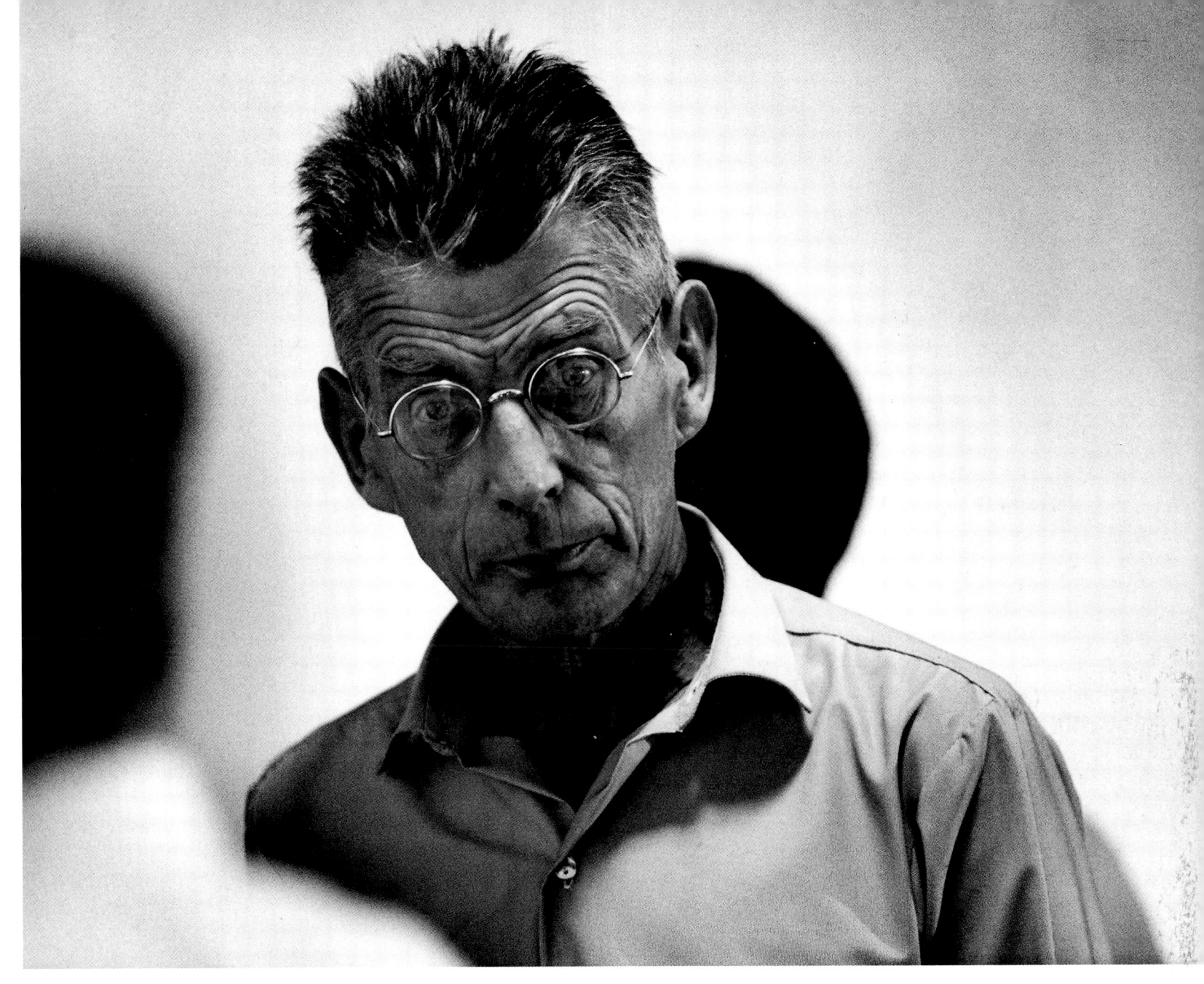

SAMUEL BECKETT *Bruce Davidson 1964*

WILLIAM FAULKNER *Henri Cartier-Bresson 1947*

BORIS PASTERNAK *Cornell Capa 1958*

134

BETTY FRIEDAN *Gilles Peress 1976*

COLETTE Henri *Cartier-Bresson 1946*

TRUMAN CAPOTE *Henri Cartier-Bresson 1946*

JACK KEROUAC *Elliott Erwitt*

JORGE LUIS BORGES *Ferdinando Scianna 1984*

NAGIB MAHFUZ *Chris Steele-Perkins 1989*

140

AYATOLLAH KHOMEINI *Abbas 1979*

AYATOLLAH KHOMEINI *Abbas 1979*

COLONEL GADDAFI WITH ALI BHUTTO & KING FAISAL *Abbas 1974*

SHAH OF IRAN *Abbas 1977*

147

YASSER ARAFAT *Abbas 1988*

HAFIZ AL ASSAD *Abbas 1976*

COLONEL GADDAFI *Abbas 1988*

Previous page: US TROOPS, KUWAIT *Bruno Barbey 1991*

SEAN CONNERY AS JAMES BOND *George Rodger 1964*

GUNMAN,
BELFAST *Gilles Peress 1972*

156

EDWARD HEATH *Jean Gaumy*

IAN PAISLEY *Gilles Peress 1979*

WINSTON CHURCHILL *Mark Riboud 1954*

Overleaf: WINSTON CHURCHILL *George Rodger (LIFE Magazine © Time Inc.) 1945*

BRITISH NAVAL OFFICER *Eugene Smith 1943*

Overleaf: BEREAVED WOMAN, CYPRUS *Don McCullin 1964*

SHELL SHOCKED G.I., VIETNAM *Don McCullin 1968*

KLAUS BARBIE *Marc Riboud 1987*

ALBERT EINSTEIN *Ernst Haas 1951*

JULIUS OPPENHEIMER *Henri Cartier-Bresson 1958*

STEPHEN HAWKING *Ian Berry 1987*

ANDREI SAKHAROV *Susan Meiselas 1977*

ALFRED KRUPP *Burt Glinn 1958*

GIOVANNI AGNELLI *Burt Glinn 1978*

LUDWIG ERHARD *Dennis Stock 1963*

J PAUL GETTY *Cornell Capa 1960*

176

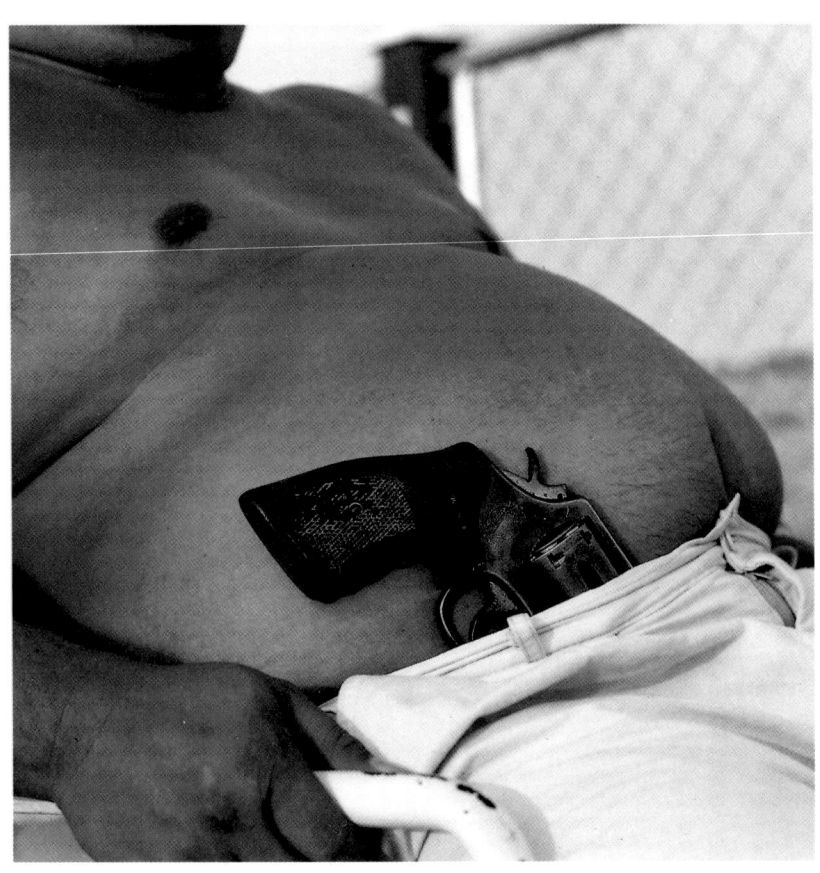

YAKUZA, JAPAN *Alberto Venzago 1989*

YAKUZA, JAPAN *Alberto Venzago 1988*

MAFIA TRIAL *Franco Zecchin 1983*

Opposite: VICTIM OF BHOPAL CHEMICAL TRAGEDY *Raghu Rai 1984*

EMPEROR HIROHITO OF JAPAN *Werner Bischof 1951*

CHIANG KAI-SHEK *Robert Capa 1938*

CHOU EN-LAI *Robert Capa 1938*

185

CHIANG & MADAME KAI-SHEK & VINEGAR JOE STILLWELL *George Rodger 1942*

MAO TSE-TUNG *Marc Riboud 1957*

HO CHI MINH *Marc Riboud 1968*

ANTI-WAR PROTESTOR & US NATIONAL GUARDSMEN *Marc Riboud 1967*

DENG XIAOPING *New China Pictures 1984*

TIENANMEN SQUARE *Stuart Franklin 1989*

MOHAMMAD ALI *Thomas Hoepker 1966*

BOB DYLAN *Danny Lyon 1962*

THE BEATLES *Don McCullin 1968*

BILLIE HOLLIDAY *Dennis Stock 1958*

JANIS JOPLIN *Elliott Landy 1969*

ELLA FITZGERALD *Dennis Stock 1958*

LUCIANO PAVAROTTI *Peter Marlow 1989*

JUDY GARLAND *Ernst Haas 1952*

YEHUDI MENUHIN *Abbas 1973*

PABLO CASALS' CELLO *Elliott Erwitt 1969*

LOUIS ARMSTRONG *Dennis Stock 1958*

LEONARD BERNSTEIN *Bruce Davidson 1958*

HERBERT VON KARAJAN *Erich Lessing 1957*

IGOR STRAVINSKY *Henri Cartier-Bresson*

ARTURO TOSCANINI *David Seymour 1954*

205

MARLENE DIETRICH *Eve Arnold 1952*

JOSEPHINE BAKER *Eve Arnold 1950*

206

THE DUKE OF EDINBURGH & QUEEN ELIZABETH II *Cornell Capa 1957*

Overleaf: SALVADOR DALI *Philippe Halsman 1948*

DUKE & DUCHESS OF WINDSOR *Philippe Halsman 1958*

MARCEL DUCHAMP *Henri Cartier-Bresson 1965*

ALBERTO GIACOMETTI *Henri Cartier-Bresson 1961*

BERNARD BERENSON *David Seymour 1955*

JEAN COCTEAU *Philippe Halsman 1949*

HENRI MATISSE *Robert Capa 1950*

PABLO PICASSO *Robert Capa 1951*

219

FRANCIS BACON *Ian Berry 1967*

ANDY WARHOL *Bob Adelman 1966*

221

ALEXANDER CALDER *Henri Cartier-Bresson 1970*

LE CORBUSIER *René Burri 1959*

WALTER GROPIUS *Burt Glinn 1958*

FRANK LLOYD WRIGHT *Werner Bischof 1953*

FRANÇOIS MITTERRAND *Guy Le Querrec 1980*

VACLAV HAVEL *Garik Pinkassov 1988*

BERLIN *James Nachtwey 1989*

TIENANMEN SQUARE *Stuart Franklin 1989*

231